HOLIDAY HISTORY
RAMADAN AND EID AL-FITR

by Marzieh A. Ali

Ideas for Parents and Teachers

Pogo Books let children practice reading informational text while introducing them to nonfiction features such as headings, labels, sidebars, maps, and diagrams, as well as a table of contents, glossary, and index.

Carefully leveled text with a strong photo match offers early fluent readers the support they need to succeed.

Before Reading

- "Walk" through the book and point out the various nonfiction features. Ask the student what purpose each feature serves.
- Look at the glossary together. Read and discuss the words.

Read the Book

- Have the child read the book independently.
- Invite him or her to list questions that arise from reading.

After Reading

- Discuss the child's questions. Talk about how he or she might find answers to those questions.
- Prompt the child to think more. Ask: The star and crescent moon are symbols of Ramadan. What do they symbolize?

Pogo Books are published by Jump!
5357 Penn Avenue South
Minneapolis, MN 55419
www.jumplibrary.com

Copyright © 2024 Jump!
International copyright reserved in all countries.
No part of this book may be reproduced in any form without written permission from the publisher.

Library of Congress Cataloging-in-Publication Data

Names: Abbas, Marzieh, author.
Title: Ramadan and Eid al-Fitr / by Marzieh A. Ali.
Description: Minneapolis, MN: Jump!, Inc., 2024.
Series: Holiday history | Includes index.
Audience: Ages 7-10
Identifiers: LCCN 2022058564 (print)
LCCN 2022058565 (ebook)
ISBN 9798885244633 (hardcover)
ISBN 9798885244640 (paperback)
ISBN 9798885244657 (ebook)
Subjects: LCSH: Ramadan—Juvenile literature.
'Īd al-Fiṭr—Juvenile literature. | Fasts and feasts—Islam—Juvenile literature.
Classification: LCC BP186.4 .A134 2024 (print)
LCC BP186.4 (ebook)
DDC 297.3/62—dc23/eng/20221215
LC record available at https://lccn.loc.gov/2022058564
LC ebook record available at https://lccn.loc.gov/2022058565

Editor: Eliza Leahy
Designer: Molly Ballanger

Photo Credits: Shutterstock, cover; arapix/iStock, 1; Mohannad Al-nahlawi/Shutterstock, 3; Mohd saidi/Shutterstock, 4; Ozbalci/iStock, 5; Odua Images/Shutterstock, 6-7; kalender/iStock, 8; FatCamera/iStock, 9; Marwani22/iStock, 10-11; Maria Fedotova/Getty, 12-13; faidzzainal/iStock, 14-15; Anadolu Agency/Getty, 16; StockImageFactory.com/Shutterstock, 17; alkang/Shutterstock, 18-19; asmiphotoshop/Shutterstock, 19; PeopleImages/iStock, 20-21; MidoSemsem/Shutterstock, 23.

Printed in the United States of America at Corporate Graphics in North Mankato, Minnesota.

TABLE OF CONTENTS

CHAPTER 1
A Month of Fasting....................4

CHAPTER 2
Ramadan Traditions....................8

CHAPTER 3
Ramadan Around the World....................16

QUICK FACTS & TOOLS
Ramadan Place of Origin....................22
Quick Facts....................22
Glossary....................23
Index....................24
To Learn More....................24

CHAPTER 1

A MONTH OF FASTING

Islam is a religion practiced by Muslims. They believe in one god, Allah. The Islamic **holy** book is the Quran.

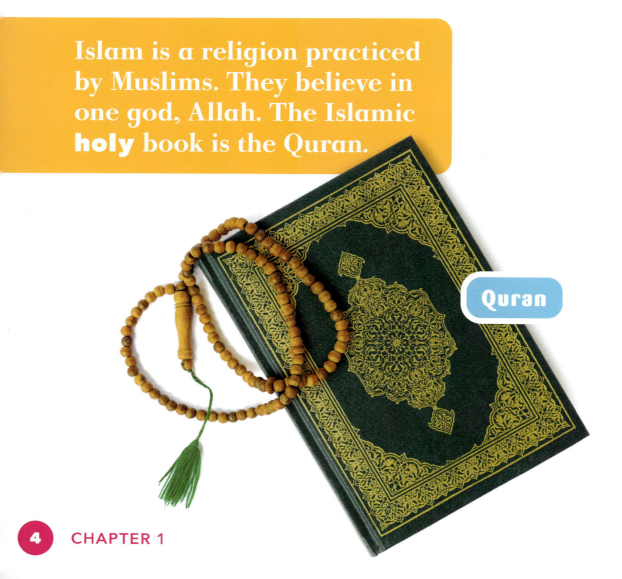

Quran

Ramadan is the ninth month of the Islamic lunar calendar. This calendar follows the Moon's **cycle**. This means the dates of Ramadan change each year.

CHAPTER 1

More than 1,400 years ago, the **Prophet** Muhammad received the first verses of the Quran. They were sent by Allah through the angel Gabriel.

Allah told Muslims to **fast** from **dawn** to **dusk** during Ramadan. At dusk, the Prophet drank water. He ate dates. Muslims still follow this **tradition** today.

WHAT DO YOU THINK?

Very young, old, or ill Muslims do not need to fast. Why do you think this is?

CHAPTER 1

CHAPTER 2
RAMADAN TRADITIONS

Before dawn on each day of Ramadan, Muslims have a meal. It is called suhoor. It includes eggs, bread, and kebabs.

After dawn, Muslims fast. Adults go to work. Children go to school. They go about their days without food or drink. After dusk, they have another meal. It is called iftar. They eat dates, broth, and fruit. They drink water and yogurt drinks.

CHAPTER 2

Ramadan is a time to help. People share with those in need. They give food, clothing, and shoes. Children collect money to donate.

It is also a time to pray and **reflect**. People go to **mosques**. They read the Quran. They talk about Islam.

WHAT DO YOU THINK?

There are five **pillars** of Islam. They are:
1. believing in one god, Allah
2. praying to Allah
3. fasting during Ramadan
4. giving to those in need
5. journeying to **Mecca**

Why do you think these pillars are important to Muslims?

People cook food for others. Children make paper lanterns. Families decorate their homes. They hang lanterns and star lights.

TAKE A LOOK!

What are some Ramadan **symbols** and their meanings? Take a look!

CRESCENT MOON AND STAR

the nights of Ramadan spent in **worship** of Allah

the start and end of Ramadan and Eid al-Fitr

LANTERN
light and **guidance**

PRAYER HANDS
praying for peace

DATES
the importance of fasting

CHAPTER 2 13

When Ramadan is over, Muslims celebrate. Eid al-Fitr marks the end of the month. It lasts three days.

People wear colorful clothing. They gather. They pray. There is a big feast.

DID YOU KNOW?

During Eid al-Fitr, adults give children money. Sometimes they give clothing, books, or toys. The gifts are called Eidi.

CHAPTER 2   **15**

CHAPTER 3
RAMADAN AROUND THE WORLD

Ramadan is a time to pray, give, and reflect. In many Arab countries, a drummer walks the streets each morning. His drumming wakes people for suhoor.

Muslims around the world celebrate Eid al-Fitr, too. People in India and Pakistan eat biryani. This is a rice and meat dish. They eat fried pastries called samosas.

biryani

CHAPTER 3 17

People cook special sweets. In Egypt, people make baklava. It is a pastry dessert. Indians and Pakistanis make a sweet pudding. It is called seviyan.

seviyan

CHAPTER 3

Muslims celebrate Eid al-Fitr with their families. They stay home from school and work. What holidays do you celebrate? Would you like to celebrate Eid al-Fitr?

CHAPTER 3   21

QUICK FACTS & TOOLS

RAMADAN PLACE OF ORIGIN

QUICK FACTS

Ramadan Dates: ninth month of the Islamic lunar calendar

Eid al-Fitr Dates: first three days of the tenth month of the Islamic lunar calendar

Year of Origin: 623 CE

Place of Origin: Madinah, Saudi Arabia

Common Symbols: crescent moon, star, lantern, Quran, prayer hands, Ramadan drum

Foods: dates, biryani, samosas, kebabs, seviyan, baklava, chai

Traditions: praying, donating to those in need, reading the Quran, decorating with lanterns, wearing colorful clothing

22 QUICK FACTS & TOOLS

GLOSSARY

cycle: A series of events that repeats in the same order.

dawn: The time of day before sunrise when light first appears in the sky.

dusk: The time of day after sunset when it starts getting dark.

fast: To stop drinking and eating all or particular foods for a time.

guidance: Advice or information meant to resolve a problem.

holy: Related to or belonging to a god or higher being.

Mecca: A holy city in Saudi Arabia that is a destination for Muslims.

mosques: Buildings where Muslims worship.

pillars: Important parts of something.

prophet: A person who speaks or claims to speak for a god.

reflect: To think carefully or seriously about something.

symbols: Objects or designs that stand for, suggest, or represent something else.

tradition: A custom, idea, or belief that is handed down from one generation to the next.

worship: To show respect to a god.

QUICK FACTS & TOOLS

INDEX

Allah 4, 6, 11, 13
clothing 11, 15
dates 6, 9, 13
dawn 6, 8, 9
drummer 16
dusk 6, 9
Egypt 19
Eid al-Fitr 13, 15, 17, 20
fast 6, 9, 11, 13
feast 15
Gabriel 6
give 11, 15, 16
iftar 9

India 17, 19
lanterns 12, 13
lunar calendar 5
money 11, 15
Moon 5, 13
mosques 11
Pakistan 17, 19
pray 11, 13, 15, 16
Prophet Muhammad 6
Quran 4, 6, 11
star 12, 13
suhoor 8, 16
tradition 6

TO LEARN MORE

Finding more information is as easy as 1, 2, 3.
 ❶ Go to www.factsurfer.com
 ❷ Enter "RamadanandEidal-Fitr" into the search box.
 ❸ Choose your book to see a list of websites.

QUICK FACTS & TOOLS